Quick and Tasty Tofu Marinades

Easy and Healthy Tofu Marinade Recipes Vegan and Vegetarian Friendly Cookbook

By: Diana Cook

Copyright © 2016 by Diana Cook

All rights reserved. This book or any portion thereof may not be reproduced or used in any manner whatsoever without the express written permission of the publisher except for the use of brief quotations in a book review.

Published in the United States of America

DOR.271-29-A

Recipe List

Cajun Asian Tofu Marinade 6

Sriracha Ahava 7

Pumpkin Peanut Tofu 8

Heidgerken 9

Tofu Fonnesbeck 10

Indian Ocean Coconut Tofu 11

Jurassic Tofu 12

Shaw City Tofu 13

Joanna's Y2K Tofu 14

Major Kane's Spicy Tofu 15

Huel's Breaded Tofu 16

Tofu Brighton 17

Spicy Peanut Tofu 18

BBQ Taco Tofu 19

Swedish Tofu 20

Red Circle Meltdown Tofu 21

Oklahoma Tofu 22

Tofu Merkle 23

Bosher's Tofu Slam 24

Graffeo 25

Arosemena 26

Tofu Rodriguez 27

Tricky Dick's Superhero Tofu 28

Vonruden 29

Kitalaroo Tofu Bricks 30

Blacksmith Tofu Vindaloo	31
Ronin Tofu	32
Clocktower Tofu	33
Annabelle's Magical Tofu Cubes	34
Mercenary Tofu	35
Riksaw Tofu	36
Tofu Samurai	37
Flower's Green Curry Tofu	38
Tuia-Ronda	39
Serisky	40
Mountain Crest Tofu Blocks	41
Soderblom	42
Schachtenzon	43
Honey Wine Tofu	44
Lemon-Lime Barbecue Tofu	45
Tomato Wyvern Tofu	46
Tofu Obermoeller	47
Pineapple and Maple Tofu	48
Destiny Tofu	49
Sorellia's Tofu Cubes	50
Tofu Kemper	51
Gideon's End of the World Tofu Slices	52
Libuttia	53
Rey's Lemon Tofu	54
Svenningsitara	55
Irish Blackened Tofu	56

Kirkland Tofu 57
Soccer Park Tofu Slices 58
World War Tofu 59

Cajun Asian Tofu Marinade

¼ cup soy sauce

1 tablespoon sesame seeds

1 ½ teaspoons ginger root, minced

1 tablespoon honey

1 tablespoon cajun seasoning

1 teaspoon juniper berries, ground

1 teaspoon black pepper

Directions:

1. In a small bowl mix together your ingredients.

2. Cover tofu and refrigerate overnight, or minimum 3 hours.

3. Cook tofu over high heat until each side is brown and crispy (about 4 minutes per side.) Use extra marinade as basting sauce.

Sriracha Ahava

¼ cup soy sauce

2 tablespoons sesame oil

2 tablespoons thyme

2 tablespoons sriracha hot sauce sauce

1 tablespoon garlic pepper

1 tablespoon celery seed (ground)

1 teaspoon black pepper

Directions:

1. In a small bowl mix together your ingredients.

2. Cover tofu and refrigerate overnight, or minimum 3 hours.

3. Cook tofu over high heat until each side is brown and crispy (about 4 minutes per side.) Use extra marinade as basting sauce.

Pumpkin Peanut Tofu

½ cup creamy peanut butter

½ cup hot water

2 tablespoons vinegar

3 tablespoons soy sauce

1 ½ tablespoons molasses

3 tablespoons pumpkin pie spice

1 tablespoon turmeric

1 tablespoon all-purpose barbeque seasoning

1 tablespoon black pepper

Directions:

1. In a small bowl mix together your ingredients.

2. Cover tofu and refrigerate overnight, or minimum 3 hours.

3. Cook tofu over high heat until each side is brown and crispy (about 4 minutes per side.) Use extra marinade as basting sauce.

Heidgerken

½ cup soy sauce

½ cup lime juice

2 tablespoons garam masala

2 tablespoons dry nacho seasoning

1 tablespoon Montreal steak spice

1 tablespoon black pepper

Directions:

1. In a small bowl mix together your ingredients.

2. Cover tofu and refrigerate overnight, or minimum 3 hours.

3. Cook tofu over high heat until each side is brown and crispy (about 4 minutes per side.) Use extra marinade as basting sauce.

Tofu Fonnesbeck

¼ cup hoisin sauce

2 tablespoons lemon juice

2 tablespoons vegan mayonnaise

1 tablespoon all-purpose seafood seasoning

1 tablespoons dill weed

2 teaspoons black pepper

Directions:

1. In a small bowl mix together your ingredients.

2. Cover tofu and refrigerate overnight, or minimum 3 hours.

3. Cook tofu over high heat until each side is brown and crispy (about 4 minutes per side.) Use extra marinade as basting sauce.

Indian Ocean Coconut Tofu

1 (14 ounce) coconut milk

¼ cup soy sauce

½ teaspoon brown sugar

1 ½ teaspoons curry powder

1 teaspoon minced fresh ginger

2 teaspoons chile paste

2 teaspoons all-purpose beef seasoning

2 teaspoons fennel seeds

1 teaspoons garlic salt

1 teaspoons honey

1 teaspoons black pepper

1 teaspoons salt

Directions:

1. In a small bowl mix together your ingredients.

2. Cover tofu and refrigerate overnight, or minimum 3 hours.

3. Cook tofu over high heat until each side is brown and crispy (about 4 minutes per side.) Use extra marinade as basting sauce.

Jurassic Tofu

1 tablespoon fresh ginger root, minced

2 tablespoons red curry paste

1 tablespoon sumac, ground

1 teaspoon white pepper

3 tablespoons lime juice

3 tablespoons soy sauce

2 tablespoons maple syrup

1 (14 ounce) can coconut milk

1 tablespoon paprika

Directions:

1. In a small bowl mix together your ingredients.

2. Cover tofu and refrigerate overnight, or minimum 3 hours.

3. Cook tofu over high heat until each side is brown and crispy (about 4 minutes per side.) Use extra marinade as basting sauce.

Shaw City Tofu

¼ cup soy sauce

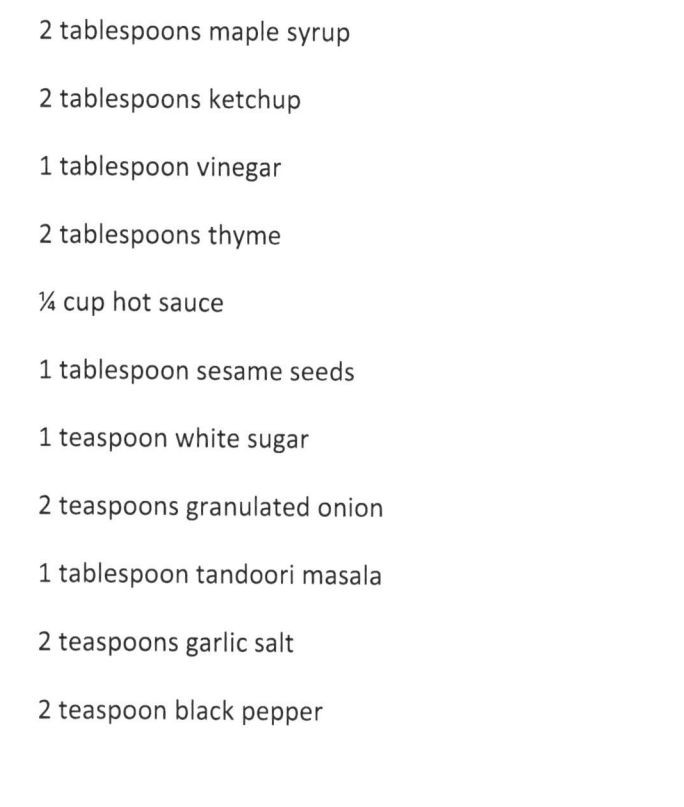

2 tablespoons maple syrup

2 tablespoons ketchup

1 tablespoon vinegar

2 tablespoons thyme

¼ cup hot sauce

1 tablespoon sesame seeds

1 teaspoon white sugar

2 teaspoons granulated onion

1 tablespoon tandoori masala

2 teaspoons garlic salt

2 teaspoon black pepper

Directions:

1. In a small bowl mix together your ingredients.

2. Cover tofu and refrigerate overnight, or minimum 3 hours.

3. Cook tofu over high heat until each side is brown and crispy (about 4 minutes per side.) Use extra marinade as basting sauce.

Joanna's Y2K Tofu

1/3 cup hot water

3 tablespoons white vinegar

3 tablespoons soy sauce

3 cloves garlic, minced

1 tablespoon brown sugar

1 teaspoon cardamom (ground)

1 teaspoon garlic pepper

2 teaspoons white pepper

2 teaspoons aniseed

2 teaspoons juniper berries, ground

Directions:

1. In a small bowl mix together your ingredients.

2. Cover tofu and refrigerate overnight, or minimum 3 hours.

3. Cook tofu over high heat until each side is brown and crispy (about 4 minutes per side.) Use extra marinade as basting sauce.

Major Kane's Spicy Tofu

1 tablespoon canola oil

1 tablespoon margarine

1 small onion, chopped

3 cloves garlic, minced

1 (10 ounce) can coconut milk

3 tablespoons hot curry powder

1 teaspoon lemon zest (grated)

1 tablespoon serrano chile powder

Directions:

1. In a small bowl mix together your ingredients.

2. Cover tofu and refrigerate overnight, or minimum 3 hours.

3. Cook tofu over high heat until each side is brown and crispy (about 4 minutes per side.) Use extra marinade as basting sauce.

Huel's Breaded Tofu

2 cups vegetable broth

3 tablespoons vegetable oil

½ cup all-purpose flour

1 teaspoon sage

½ teaspoon cayenne pepper

1 tablespoon all-purpose seafood seasoning

1 tablespoon aniseed

1 teaspoon black pepper

1 teaspoon salt

Directions:

1. In a small bowl mix together your ingredients.

2. Cover tofu and refrigerate overnight, or minimum 3 hours.

3. Cook tofu over high heat until each side is brown and crispy (about 4 minutes per side.) Use extra marinade as basting sauce.

Tofu Brighton

1 tablespoon vegetable oil

1 onion, chopped

½ cup soy sauce

1 (14 ounce) can creamed corn

2 tablespoons curry paste

1 tablespoon thyme

1 teaspoon cloves (ground)

1 tablespoon bay leaves (ground)

1 tablespoon sumac (ground)

Directions:

1. In a small bowl mix together your ingredients.

2. Cover tofu and refrigerate overnight, or minimum 3 hours.

3. Cook tofu over high heat until each side is brown and crispy (about 4 minutes per side.) Use extra marinade as basting sauce.

Spicy Peanut Tofu

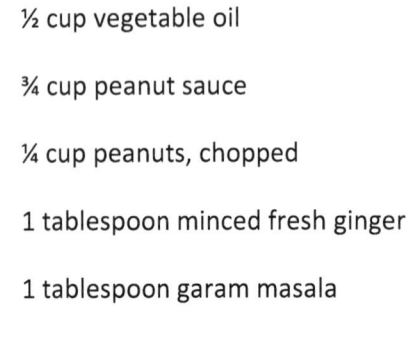

½ cup vegetable oil

¾ cup peanut sauce

¼ cup peanuts, chopped

1 tablespoon minced fresh ginger

1 tablespoon garam masala

1 tablespoon paprika

2 teaspoons cayenne pepper

2 teaspoons granulated garlic

2 teaspoons lavender

2 teaspoons juniper berries (ground)

2 teaspoons black pepper

2 teaspoons salt

Directions:

1. In a small bowl mix together your ingredients.

2. Cover tofu and refrigerate overnight, or minimum 3 hours.

3. Cook tofu over high heat until each side is brown and crispy (about 4 minutes per side.) Use extra marinade as basting sauce.

BBQ Taco Tofu

1 cup barbeque sauce

3 tablespoons olive oil

1 tablespoon nutmeg

1 tablespoon onion salt

1 tablespoon garlic salt

2 tablespoons celery seed (ground)

4 tablespoons taco seasoning mix

2 tablespoons turmeric

1 tablespoon sea salt/kosher salt

Directions:

1. In a small bowl mix together your ingredients.

2. Cover tofu and refrigerate overnight, or minimum 3 hours.

3. Cook tofu over high heat until each side is brown and crispy (about 4 minutes per side.) Use extra marinade as basting sauce.

Swedish Tofu

1/3 cup soy sauce

1/3 cup maple syrup

1 tablespoon rosemary

1 tablespoon lemon pepper

1 tablespoon savory (ground)

1 tablespoon taco seasoning mix

2 tablespoons all-purpose beef seasoning

2 tablespoons black pepper

Directions:

1. In a small bowl mix together your ingredients.

2. Cover tofu and refrigerate overnight, or minimum 3 hours.

3. Cook tofu over high heat until each side is brown and crispy (about 4 minutes per side.) Use extra marinade as basting sauce.

Red Circle Meltdown Tofu

¼ cup whiskey

1/3 cup barbecue sauce

2 tablespoons pineapple juice

2 tablespoons cayenne pepper

1 tablespoon all-purpose beef seasoning

1 tablespoon garam masala

1 tablespoon lavender

1 tablespoon black pepper

1 tablespoon sea salt/kosher salt

Directions:

1. In a small bowl mix together your ingredients.

2. Cover tofu and refrigerate overnight, or minimum 3 hours.

3. Cook tofu over high heat until each side is brown and crispy (about 4 minutes per side.) Use extra marinade as basting sauce.

Oklahoma Tofu

1 tablespoon vegetable oil

½ cup water

4 tablespoons rice wine vinegar

2 tablespoons honey

2 tablespoons soy sauce

2 tablespoons onion salt

2 tablespoons paprika

2 tablespoons maple sugar/syrup

1 tablespoon black pepper

1 tablespoon sea salt/kosher salt

Directions:

1. In a small bowl mix together your ingredients.

2. Cover tofu and refrigerate overnight, or minimum 3 hours.

3. Cook tofu over high heat until each side is brown and crispy (about 4 minutes per side.) Use extra marinade as basting sauce.

Tofu Merkle

½ cup soy sauce

3 tablespoons maple syrup

3 tablespoons ketchup

1 tablespoon vinegar

2 tablespoons savory (ground)

1 tablespoon all-purpose beef seasoning

2 tablespoons dill weed

2 tablespoons marjoram

2 tablespoons black pepper

1 tablespoon sea salt/kosher salt

Directions:

1. In a small bowl mix together your ingredients.

2. Cover tofu and refrigerate overnight, or minimum 3 hours.

3. Cook tofu over high heat until each side is brown and crispy (about 4 minutes per side.) Use extra marinade as basting sauce.

Bosher's Tofu Slam

3 tablespoons margarine, melted

¼ cup dry white wine

2 cubes vegetable bouillon

¼ cup prepared mustard

1/3 cup honey

1 cup water

2 tablespoons cayenne pepper

2 tablespoons aniseed

1 tablespoon cornmeal

1 tablespoon black pepper

1 tablespoon salt

Directions:

1. In a small bowl mix together your ingredients.

2. Cover tofu and refrigerate overnight, or minimum 3 hours.

3. Cook tofu over high heat until each side is brown and crispy (about 4 minutes per side.) Use extra marinade as basting sauce.

Graffeo

½ cup apple juice

½ cup vegan mayonnaise

1 tablespoon dry beef soup mix

2 tablespoons sage

1 tablespoon coriander seed (ground)

1 tablespoon marjoram

1 tablespoon jalapeno powder

2 tablespoons dill seeds (ground)

2 tablespoons black pepper

Directions:

1. In a small bowl mix together your ingredients.

2. Cover tofu and refrigerate overnight, or minimum 3 hours.

3. Cook tofu over high heat until each side is brown and crispy (about 4 minutes per side.) Use extra marinade as basting sauce.

Arosemena

1/3 cup dark beer

¼ cup soy sauce

1 tablespoon Chinese five-spice powder

1 tablespoon garlic pepper

2 tablespoons coriander seed (ground)

2 tablespoons cumin

1 tablespoon black pepper

1 tablespoon sea salt

Directions:

1. In a small bowl mix together your ingredients.

2. Cover tofu and refrigerate overnight, or minimum 3 hours.

3. Cook tofu over high heat until each side is brown and crispy (about 4 minutes per side.) Use extra marinade as basting sauce.

Tofu Rodriguez

3 tablespoons lime juice

3 tablespoons soy sauce

2 tablespoons maple syrup

1 (14 ounce) can coconut milk

2 tablespoons fajita seasoning mix

1 tablespoon oregano

1 tablespoon dill weed

2 tablespoons garlic salt

2 tablespoons black pepper

Directions:

1. In a small bowl mix together your ingredients.

2. Cover tofu and refrigerate overnight, or minimum 3 hours.

3. Cook tofu over high heat until each side is brown and crispy (about 4 minutes per side.) Use extra marinade as basting sauce.

Tricky Dick's Superhero Tofu

½ cup almond milk

¼ cup soy sauce

¼ cup cranberry juice

1 tablespoon burrito seasoning mix

1 tablespoon hot chili powder

1 tablespoon cornmeal

2 tablespoons coffee beans (ground)

1 tablespoon sesame seeds

2 tablespoons black pepper

1 tablespoon sea salt/kosher salt

Directions:

1. In a small bowl mix together your ingredients.

2. Cover tofu and refrigerate overnight, or minimum 3 hours.

3. Cook tofu over high heat until each side is brown and crispy (about 4 minutes per side.) Use extra marinade as basting sauce.

Vonruden

1 (14 ounce) can coconut milk

½ cup vegetable broth

2 tablespoons all-purpose Greek seasoning

1 tablespoon Montreal steak spice

1 tablespoon tandoori masala

1 tablespoon garlic powder

2 tablespoons all-purpose seafood seasoning

Directions:

1. In a small bowl mix together your ingredients.

2. Cover tofu and refrigerate overnight, or minimum 3 hours.

3. Cook tofu over high heat until each side is brown and crispy (about 4 minutes per side.) Use extra marinade as basting sauce.

Kitalaroo Tofu Bricks

2 tablespoons hoisin sauce

1/3 cup coconut milk

1/3 cup soy sauce

3 cloves garlic, minced

2 tablespoons tandoori masala

1 tablespoon onion salt

1 tablespoon coriander powder

2 tablespoons hot curry powder

1 tablespoon black pepper

Directions:

1. In a small bowl mix together your ingredients.

2. Cover tofu and refrigerate overnight, or minimum 3 hours.

3. Cook tofu over high heat until each side is brown and crispy (about 4 minutes per side.) Use extra marinade as basting sauce.

Blacksmith Tofu Vindaloo

1 (15 ounce) can coconut milk

1 cup vegetable broth

3 tablespoons vindaloo curry powder

6 tablespoons tomato paste

1 tablespoon cinnamon

1 tablespoon taco seasoning mix

2 tablespoons jalapeno powder powder

1 tablespoon granulated garlic

1 tablespoon black pepper

1 tablespoon sea salt/kosher salt

Directions:

1. In a small bowl mix together your ingredients.

2. Cover tofu and refrigerate overnight, or minimum 3 hours.

3. Cook tofu over high heat until each side is brown and crispy (about 4 minutes per side.) Use extra marinade as basting sauce.

Ronin Tofu

1/3 cup vegan mayonnaise

1/3 cup mustard

1 teaspoon saffron

1 tablespoon bay leaves (ground)

2 tablespoons dill weed

2 tablespoons dry vegetarian soup mix

1 tablespoon coriander powder

1 tablespoon black pepper

1 tablespoon salt

Directions:

1. In a small bowl mix together your ingredients.

2. Cover tofu and refrigerate overnight, or minimum 3 hours.

3. Cook tofu over high heat until each side is brown and crispy (about 4 minutes per side.) Use extra marinade as basting sauce.

Clocktower Tofu

Juice of 1 fresh lime

3 tablespoons canola oil

2 teaspoons garlic, minced

2 teaspoons fresh ginger root, minced

1 teaspoon mint leaves (ground)

1 teaspoon hot chili powder

1 teaspoon aniseed

1 tablespoon soy sauce

Directions:

1. In a small bowl mix together your ingredients.

2. Cover tofu and refrigerate overnight, or minimum 3 hours.

3. Cook tofu over high heat until each side is brown and crispy (about 4 minutes per side.) Use extra marinade as basting sauce.

Annabelle's Magical Tofu Cubes

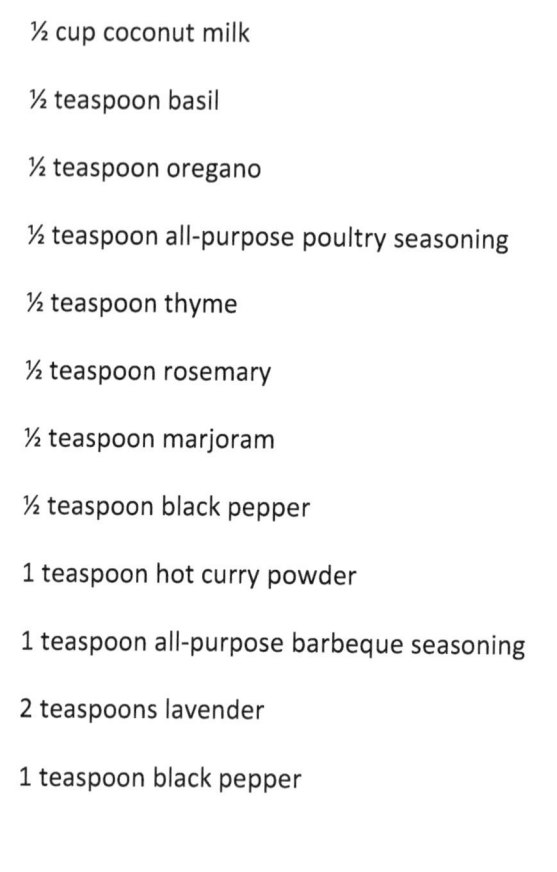

½ cup coconut milk

½ teaspoon basil

½ teaspoon oregano

½ teaspoon all-purpose poultry seasoning

½ teaspoon thyme

½ teaspoon rosemary

½ teaspoon marjoram

½ teaspoon black pepper

1 teaspoon hot curry powder

1 teaspoon all-purpose barbeque seasoning

2 teaspoons lavender

1 teaspoon black pepper

Directions:

1. In a small bowl mix together your ingredients.

2. Cover tofu and refrigerate overnight, or minimum 3 hours.

3. Cook tofu over high heat until each side is brown and crispy (about 4 minutes per side.) Use extra marinade as basting sauce.

Mercenary Tofu

1/3 cup soy sauce

1 teaspoon chili powder

2 cloves garlic, minced

2 tablespoons vegetable oil

1/2 cup onion, chopped

1 teaspoon white sugar

1 teaspoon lemon pepper

2 teaspoon dry tomato soup mix

1 teaspoon hot curry powder

2 teaspoon black pepper

Directions:

1. In a small bowl mix together your ingredients.

2. Cover tofu and refrigerate overnight, or minimum 3 hours.

3. Cook tofu over high heat until each side is brown and crispy (about 4 minutes per side.) Use extra marinade as basting sauce.

Riksaw Tofu

1/3 cup coconut milk

1/3 cup vegan mayonnaise

2 tablespoons rosemary

1 tablespoon mace (ground)

1 tablespoon lemon pepper

1 tablespoon habanero powder

2 tablespoons sesame seeds

2 tablespoons black pepper

Directions:

1. In a small bowl mix together your ingredients.

2. Cover tofu and refrigerate overnight, or minimum 3 hours.

3. Cook tofu over high heat until each side is brown and crispy (about 4 minutes per side.) Use extra marinade as basting sauce.

Tofu Samurai

1/3 cup soy sauce

1/3 cup orange juice

1 tablespoon maple syrup

2 tablespoons caraway seeds

1 tablespoon cinnamon

1 tablespoon mint leaves (ground)

1 tablespoon hot sauce

Directions:

1. In a small bowl mix together your ingredients.

2. Cover tofu and refrigerate overnight, or minimum 3 hours.

3. Cook tofu over high heat until each side is brown and crispy (about 4 minutes per side.) Use extra marinade as basting sauce.

Flower's Green Curry Tofu

1 (10 ounce) can coconut milk

2 tablespoons green curry paste

3 tablespoons sesame oil

1 tablespoon hot curry powder

1 tablespoon tandoori paste

2 cloves garlic, minced

1 teaspoon black pepper

1 teaspoon salt

Directions:

1. In a small bowl mix together your ingredients.

2. Cover tofu and refrigerate overnight, or minimum 3 hours.

3. Cook tofu over high heat until each side is brown and crispy (about 4 minutes per side.) Use extra marinade as basting sauce.

Tuia-Ronda

¼ cup prepared mustard

1/3 cup soy sauce

1/3 cup maple syrup

1 tablespoon sumac (ground)

2 tablespoons garlic salt

2 tablespoons fennel seeds

2 tablespoons thyme

1 tablespoon black pepper

Directions:

1. In a small bowl mix together your ingredients.

2. Cover tofu and refrigerate overnight, or minimum 3 hours.

3. Cook tofu over high heat until each side is brown and crispy (about 4 minutes per side.) Use extra marinade as basting sauce.

Serisky

½ cup vegetable broth

¼ cup orange juice

1 tablespoon juniper berries (ground)

1 teaspoon saffron

1 tablespoon cayenne pepper

1 tablespoon Montreal steak spice

1 tablespoon black pepper

1 tablespoon salt

Directions:

1. In a small bowl mix together your ingredients.

2. Cover tofu and refrigerate overnight, or minimum 3 hours.

3. Cook tofu over high heat until each side is brown and crispy (about 4 minutes per side.) Use extra marinade as basting sauce.

Mountain Crest Tofu Blocks

1/3 cup peanut sauce

2 tablespoons water

2 tablespoons lime juice

2 tablespoons aniseed

2 tablespoons jalapeno powder

1 tablespoon brown sugar

1 tablespoon all-purpose chicken seasoning

1 tablespoon black pepper

1 tablespoon sea salt/kosher salt

Directions:

1. In a small bowl mix together your ingredients.

2. Cover tofu and refrigerate overnight, or minimum 3 hours.

3. Cook tofu over high heat until each side is brown and crispy (about 4 minutes per side.) Use extra marinade as basting sauce.

Soderblom

2/3 cup water

¼ cup margarine, melted

3 tablespoons vegetable oil

1 tablespoon barbeque sauce

1 tablespoon prepared mustard

1 tablespoon orange juice

1 tablespoon sesame seeds

1 tablespoon dried bread crumbs

1 tablespoon cilantro

1 tablespoon cardamom (ground)

1 tablespoon granulated garlic

2 tablespoons rosemary

Directions:

1. In a small bowl mix together your ingredients.

2. Cover tofu and refrigerate overnight, or minimum 3 hours.

3. Cook tofu over high heat until each side is brown and crispy (about 4 minutes per side.) Use extra marinade as basting sauce.

Schachtenzon

1 (16 ounce) can tomato sauce

1/3 cup vegan mayonnaise

2 tablespoons lemon juice

1 tablespoon cinnamon

2 tablespoons cilantro

1 tablespoon cayenne pepper

2 tablespoons dried bread crumbs

2 tablespoons parsley

1 tablespoon sea salt/kosher salt

Directions:

1. In a small bowl mix together your ingredients.

2. Cover tofu and refrigerate overnight, or minimum 3 hours.

3. Cook tofu over high heat until each side is brown and crispy (about 4 minutes per side.) Use extra marinade as basting sauce.

Honey Wine Tofu

½ cup white wine

½ cup vegetable broth

½ cup honey

2 tablespoons lemon zest (grated)

1 tablespoon savory (ground)

1 tablespoon maple sugar/syrup

2 tablespoons ginger (ground)

2 teaspoons black pepper

2 teaspoons salt

Directions:

1. In a small bowl mix together your ingredients.

2. Cover tofu and refrigerate overnight, or minimum 3 hours.

3. Cook tofu over high heat until each side is brown and crispy (about 4 minutes per side.) Use extra marinade as basting sauce.

Lemon-Lime Barbecue Tofu

½ cup barbecue sauce

2 tablespoons lemon juice

2 tablespoons lime juice

1 tablespoon tandoori masala

2 tablespoons cajun seasoning

1 tablespoon sage

1 tablespoon garlic salt

1 tablespoon black pepper

Directions:

1. In a small bowl mix together your ingredients.

2. Cover tofu and refrigerate overnight, or minimum 3 hours.

3. Cook tofu over high heat until each side is brown and crispy (about 4 minutes per side.) Use extra marinade as basting sauce.

Tomato Wyvern Tofu

1 tablespoon red pepper flakes

1/3 cup water

1 tablespoon tomato paste

1 cup diced tomatoes

1 tablespoon oregano

1 tablespoon basil

2 cloves garlic, minced

1 teaspoon white pepper

1 teaspoon salt

Directions:

1. In a small bowl mix together your ingredients.

2. Cover tofu and refrigerate overnight, or minimum 3 hours.

3. Cook tofu over high heat until each side is brown and crispy (about 4 minutes per side.) Use extra marinade as basting sauce.

Tofu Obermoeller

1/2 white onion, chopped

2 cloves garlic, minced

1 (6 ounce) can tomato paste

1/2 cup peanut butter

2 tablespoons caraway seeds

2 tablespoons parsley

1 tablespoon all-purpose beef seasoning

1 tablespoon black pepper

1 tablespoon salt

Directions:

1. In a small bowl mix together your ingredients.

2. Cover tofu and refrigerate overnight, or minimum 3 hours.

3. Cook tofu over high heat until each side is brown and crispy (about 4 minutes per side.) Use extra marinade as basting sauce.

Pineapple and Maple Tofu

½ cup maple syrup

½ cup pineapple juice

1 tablespoon soy sauce

2 tablespoons prepared mustard

1 tablespoon olive oil

1 tablespoon onion salt

1 tablespoon black pepper

Directions:

1. In a small bowl mix together your ingredients.

2. Cover tofu and refrigerate overnight, or minimum 3 hours.

3. Cook tofu over high heat until each side is brown and crispy (about 4 minutes per side.) Use extra marinade as basting sauce.

Destiny Tofu

1/3 cup lime juice

2 tablespoons olive oil

¼ cup fresh cilantro, chopped

3 cloves garlic, minced

2 teaspoons hot chili powder

1 tablespoon cayenne pepper

1 tablespoon maple sugar/syrup

2 tablespoons fresh ginger, grated

1 tablespoon dill seeds (ground)

1 tablespoon celery seed (ground)

1 tablespoon black pepper

Directions:

1. In a small bowl mix together your ingredients.

2. Cover tofu and refrigerate overnight, or minimum 3 hours.

3. Cook tofu over high heat until each side is brown and crispy (about 4 minutes per side.) Use extra marinade as basting sauce.

Sorellia's Tofu Cubes

½ cup soy sauce

½ cup lime juice

2 tablespoons cardamom (ground)

1 tablespoon cilantro

2 tablespoons all-purpose seafood seasoning

1 tablespoon black pepper

1 tablespoon sea salt/kosher salt

Directions:

1. In a small bowl mix together your ingredients.

2. Cover tofu and refrigerate overnight, or minimum 3 hours.

3. Cook tofu over high heat until each side is brown and crispy (about 4 minutes per side.) Use extra marinade as basting sauce.

Tofu Kemper

1/3 cup barbecue sauce

1/3 cup vegan mayonnaise

1 tablespoon cilantro

2 tablespoons monosodium glutamate (MSG)

1 tablespoon ginger (ground)

1 tablespoon garam masala

2 tablespoons black pepper

1 tablespoon sea salt/kosher salt

Directions:

1. In a small bowl mix together your ingredients.

2. Cover tofu and refrigerate overnight, or minimum 3 hours.

3. Cook tofu over high heat until each side is brown and crispy (about 4 minutes per side.) Use extra marinade as basting sauce.

Gideon's End of the World Tofu Slices

¼ cup soy sauce

¼ cup lime juice

¼ cup maple syrup

2 tablespoons minced garlic

2 tablespoons habanero powder

1 tablespoon turmeric

1 tablespoon jerk seasoning

1 tablespoon black pepper

Directions:

1. In a small bowl mix together your ingredients.

2. Cover tofu and refrigerate overnight, or minimum 3 hours.

3. Cook tofu over high heat until each side is brown and crispy (about 4 minutes per side.) Use extra marinade as basting sauce.

Libuttia

¾ cup peanut butter

2 tablespoons vegetable oil

½ cup chopped pecans

1 tablespoon cayenne pepper

2 tablespoons onion salt

1 tablespoon Chinese five-spice powder

2 tablespoons jalapeno powder

1 tablespoon black pepper

1 tablespoon sea salt/kosher salt

Directions:

1. In a small bowl mix together your ingredients.

2. Cover tofu and refrigerate overnight, or minimum 3 hours.

3. Cook tofu over high heat until each side is brown and crispy (about 4 minutes per side.) Use extra marinade as basting sauce.

Rey's Lemon Tofu

1/3 cup lemon juice

2 tablespoons pineapple juice

1 tablespoon mustard seed (ground)

1 tablespoon lemon pepper

1 tablespoon paprika

1 tablespoon sage

1 tablespoon onion salt

1 tablespoon black pepper

Directions:

1. In a small bowl mix together your ingredients.

2. Cover tofu and refrigerate overnight, or minimum 3 hours.

3. Cook tofu over high heat until each side is brown and crispy (about 4 minutes per side.) Use extra marinade as basting sauce.

Svenningsitara

1 cup vegetable broth

2 tablespoons soy sauce

2 tablespoons garlic salt

1 tablespoon all-purpose Greek seasoning

1 tablespoon jerk seasoning

2 tablespoons garam masala

Directions:

1. In a small bowl mix together your ingredients.

2. Cover tofu and refrigerate overnight, or minimum 3 hours.

3. Cook tofu over high heat until each side is brown and crispy (about 4 minutes per side.) Use extra marinade as basting sauce.

Irish Blackened Tofu

½ cup soy sauce

½ cup Guinness beer

1 tablespoon mace (ground)

1 tablespoon lemon pepper

1 tablespoon fajita seasoning mix

1 tablespoon fennel seeds

2 tablespoons sage

1 tablespoon black pepper

Directions:

1. In a small bowl mix together your ingredients.

2. Cover tofu and refrigerate overnight, or minimum 3 hours.

3. Cook tofu over high heat until each side is brown and crispy (about 4 minutes per side.) Use extra marinade as basting sauce.

Kirkland Tofu

½ cup apple juice

½ cup orange juice

½ cup soy sauce

1 tablespoon dry vegetarian soup mix

2 tablespoons mustard seed (ground)

2 tablespoons all-purpose chicken seasoning

1 tablespoon black peppercorns (coarsely ground)

2 tablespoons black pepper

Directions:

1. In a small bowl mix together your ingredients.

2. Cover tofu and refrigerate overnight, or minimum 3 hours.

3. Cook tofu over high heat until each side is brown and crispy (about 4 minutes per side.) Use extra marinade as basting sauce.

Soccer Park Tofu Slices

½ cup vegan mayonnaise

½ cup chopped fresh dill

1/3 cup prepared mustard

2 packages ranch dressing mix

1 tablespoon brown sugar

1 tablespoon cornmeal

2 tablespoons dried Italian bread crumbs

1 tablespoon black pepper

1 tablespoon sea salt/kosher salt

Directions:

1. In a small bowl mix together your ingredients.

2. Cover tofu and refrigerate overnight, or minimum 3 hours.

3. Cook tofu over high heat until each side is brown and crispy (about 4 minutes per side.) Use extra marinade as basting sauce.

World War Tofu

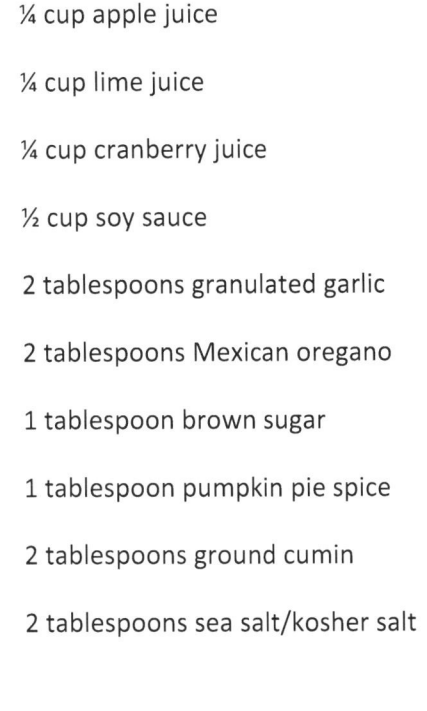

¼ cup apple juice

¼ cup lime juice

¼ cup cranberry juice

½ cup soy sauce

2 tablespoons granulated garlic

2 tablespoons Mexican oregano

1 tablespoon brown sugar

1 tablespoon pumpkin pie spice

2 tablespoons ground cumin

2 tablespoons sea salt/kosher salt

Directions:

1. In a small bowl mix together your ingredients.

2. Cover tofu and refrigerate overnight, or minimum 3 hours.

3. Cook tofu over high heat until each side is brown and crispy (about 4 minutes per side.) Use extra marinade as basting sauce.

Made in the USA
Lexington, KY
24 January 2018